SUMMARY

Review & Analysis of
Schultz and Doerr's Book

Rainmaking
Conversations

—— BusinessNews Publishing ——

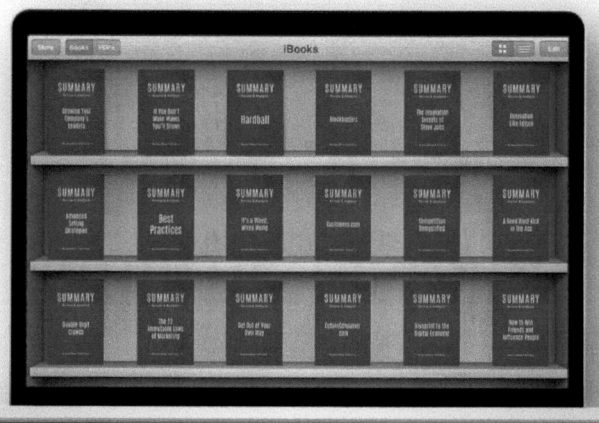

BOOK PRESENTATION *RAINMAKING CONVERSA-TIONS* BY MIKE SCHULTZ AND JOHN E. DOERR 1

SUMMARY OF *RAINMAKING CONVERSATIONS* (MIKE SCHULTZ AND JOHN E. DOERR) 4

BOOK PRESENTATION *RAINMAKING CONVERSATIONS* BY MIKE SCHULTZ AND JOHN E. DOERR

BOOK ABSTRACT

MAIN IDEA

Rainmaking conversations are sales conversations which fill the new customer pipeline, win new deals and create new opportunities for great things to happen in the future. They're based around the RAIN acronym:

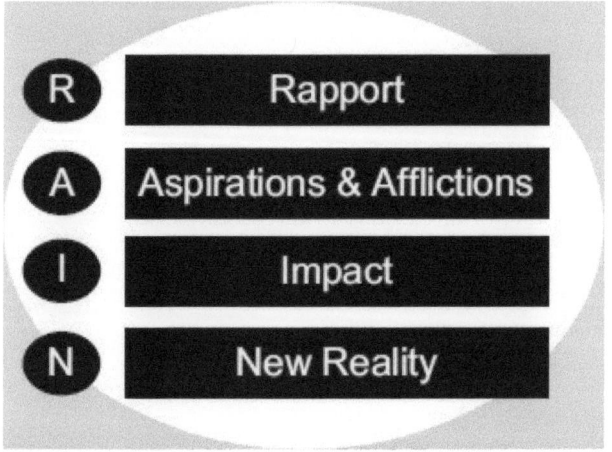

To get more sales for your firm learn how to prepare for and then have more RAIN conversations. Getting to this stage requires that you prepare well, understand the RAIN roadmap, focus on the RASP keys of rainmaking success and apply the 10 Rainmaker Principles.

> *"The RAIN acronym is also a nod to the fact this process is focused on rainmakers – a common name for people who bring the most new clients and revenue into an organization. RAIN is your guide to leading successful sales conversations."*
>
> *– Mike Schultz and John Doerr*

> *"We developed the RAIN Selling method to provide a framework, road map, and learning process for those who want to become rainmakers. Follow the Rainmaker Conversations road map and it will help you to sell effectively. But if you really want to achieve and join the rank of the rainmaker elite, you should take the 10 Rainmaker Principles to heart. Here's to the beginning of your long and fruitful journey down that path. Rainmakers have it good. Now, go out and make it RAIN."*
>
> *– Mike Schultz and John Doerr*

ABOUT THE AUTHOR

MIKE SCHULTZ is co-president of RAIN Group, a sales training organization. He works as a consultant with organizations such as John Hancock and Ryder to improve sales performance and develop rainmakers. He also teaches seminars and delivers keynotes at industry conferences as well as being on the faculty of Babson College.

JOHN DOERR is also co-president of RAIN Group. After an extensive career in business leadership, he now teaches and coaches thousands of sales professionals in many countries. In addition to working with leading organizations like London Business School, DHL and Informatica, John Doerr has sold millions of products and services to some of the world's most prestigious institutions.

The Web site for this book is at www.RainSalesTraining.com.

IMPORTANT NOTE ABOUT THIS EBOOK

This is a summary and not a critique or a review of the book. It does not offer judgment or opinion on the content of the book. This summary may not be organized chapter-wise but is an overview of the main ideas, viewpoints and arguments from the book as a whole. This means that the organization of this summary is not a representation of the book.

SUMMARY OF *RAINMAKING CONVERSATIONS* (MIKE SCHULTZ AND JOHN E. DOERR)

1. PREPARING TO HAVE RAIN CONVERSATIONS

RAIN conversations don't arise by accident. To make them happen, you've got to prepare well. The basic steps involved are:

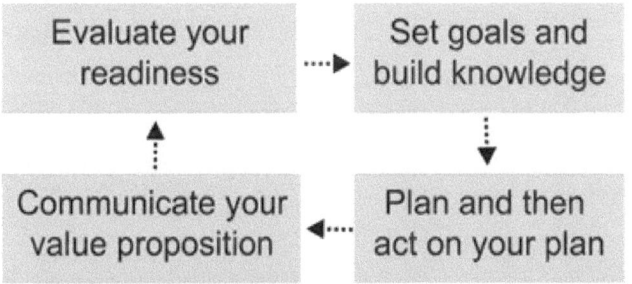

EVALUATE YOUR READINESS

To start the quest to become a rainmaker, ask yourself six questions:

1. How strong is my desire to excel in a sales role?
2. How committed am I to the principle of doing whatever it will take to succeed?
3. How much energy will I personally commit to succeeding as a rainmaker?

4. How's my attitude? Am I positive about succeeding or do negative thoughts derail my efforts to become a rainmaker even before I even begin?
5. Do I accept responsibility for the results I generate – or am I willing to just make excuses?
6. Am I willing to face my own personal sales demons – my hidden weaknesses and flaws?

Unless and until you want more success in your sales career and you're willing to do whatever it takes to get there, it's unlikely you'll become a rainmaker. Similarly, until you're ready to put in the time and effort involved to move forward, other things will always take precedence and you'll strike obstacles you never overcome. To become a rainmaker, you've got to believe you're responsible for your own success and be willing to work at what you're weak at. Rainmakers have these conversations with themselves and ask the right questions before they even embark on the journey. You'll need to do the same.

SET GOALS AND BUILD KNOWLEDGE

In a recent survey of 400,000 salespeople, the top five percent of achievers were compared to the bottom five percent. It was shown:

- 100 percent of those in the top five percent bracket had written goals.
- 16 percent of those in the bottom five percent bracket had written goals.

You won't reach rainmaker status by accident. To get there, you've got to set a written goal to be a rainmaker, live by that goal and commit whatever it takes to achieve your goal.

PLAN AND THEN ACT ON YOUR PLAN

A simple routine for acting on your intention to become a rainmaker is:

- Every day, review your goals first thing in the morning and identify what you can do to move forward.
- Take a few minutes at the end of each day to review how things went and set goals for tomorrow.
- Each Friday, review how the week went and set your goals and action plans for the coming week.
- Once a month, meet with a small group of people you trust and review how you're going.
- Once a quarter, carry out a personal review: "What do I absolutely need to do in the next three months to achieve my annual goals?" Set three priorities for the next quarter you will focus on.
- Once each year, set your targets for the coming year. "What do I need to do this year to reach my big-picture goals?" If you can, break that big yearly goal down into quarterly and monthly goals.

The whole key is if your system is simple, you're more likely to use it than if it's not. Some people just write their goals down on a piece of paper and keep it in the top drawer of their desk and this works well for them. Others have a Word file they open each week to review and update progress. Don't put off setting goals and tracking your progress until you have the "perfect" system in place. Get started on setting goals, making plans and then acting on your plans today.

COMMUNICATE YOUR VALUE PROPOSITION

To have rainmaker conversations, you first need to understand clearly the value you can provide and the impact you can have. When a new prospect meets you for the first time, you need to be able to communicate that value proposition well.

In practical terms, a value proposition is the collection of reasons why someone should buy from you. Based on your value proposition, you can then develop a positioning statement which will be a compelling, tangible statement of how any company or individual will benefit from buying from you.

A value proposition must do three things

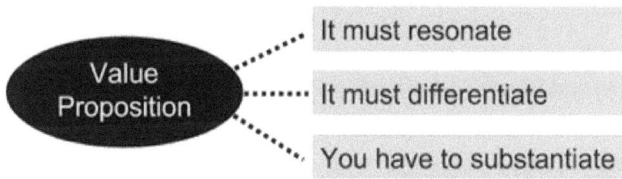

- Prospects have to want and need what you're selling because it resonates with them and addresses their key issues and concerns.
- Potential buyers have to see that you stand out from all the other available options.
- Prospects will only be interested if they believe you can deliver what you're promising with your value proposition.

To lay the foundation for engaging in RAIN conversations and to become a rainmaker, give some thought to your firm's value proposition. Make it sizzle. For example:

- "We help companies improve their sales performance. If you want your salespeople, professionals and leaders to sell more, we can help."
- "We work with some of the world's best-known companies to help them protect the value of their brands. Just last week, we helped one of our clients protect their new software from counterfeiting which safeguarded millions of dollars of future revenue for them. We'd be happy to explore helping you do something similar."

2. KEY CONCEPTS OF RAIN SELLING

The roadmap for an effective RAIN conversation is:

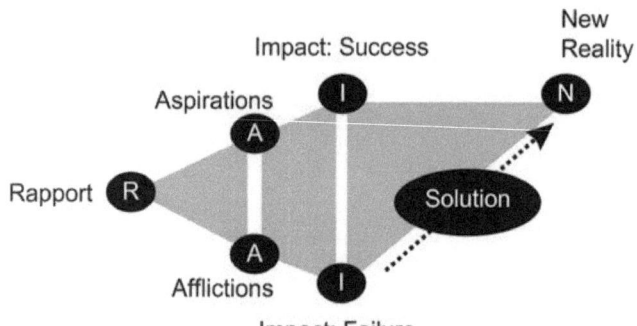

1.

Having the ability to genuinely connect with prospects sounds old fashioned but it's not. This is actually more relevant and more important than ever. Rapport isn't about forming a superficial connection with the prospect. Instead, rapport is the act of forming an authentic connection with them.

Genuine rapport sets the foundation for the rest of the conversation. It also creates an opening for trust and a strong relationship to grow and deepen. Rapport in sales is vital because – all other things being equal – people prefer to buy from someone they like. If you can develop bona fide rapport with the prospect, you just might tip the scales in your favor.

So how do you build rapport? You build it by being genuine and by asking questions which establish and then strengthen an emotional connection. The points to remember are:

- Make it your habit to be warm and friendly towards people you don't know and those you approach. They expect a chilly reaction. Surprise them by being down-to-earth and interested in what they're about. That will get things off to a good start.
- Don't "try too hard" or come across as "needy." That makes people feel uncomfortable. Only give compliments if you honestly mean them. Calibrate your level

of rapport so it is just right.

- Understand their culture. Show you respect what they stand for.
- Tell some stories which build your credibility and start people down the road of an emotional journey. People crave knowing what happens next. Feed that itch and listen to what they say for clues.
- Hit a good balance between advocacy (giving advice) and inquiry (asking questions). Make them comfortable rather than feeling like they are facing a courtroom battle.

The questions you ask should be situation specific. Depending on the other person and your relationship to them, you could ask them:

- "How was your weekend? Did you get up to anything interesting?"
- "You know, I enjoyed hearing the short version of your background when last we met. If you have a few minutes, I'd enjoy hearing the long version."
- "I have to admit right up-front I was intrigued by that piece of art in your lobby. What's the story behind that piece?"
- "Well, you're clearly new to this area. Where are you staying? What have you found different about being here compared to where you lived previously?"

The real key to building rapport is to do things you feel comfortable about. If you try and stick to a canned script, your efforts to build rapport will come across as insincere and contrived. Be yourself. Something you can try if you're struggling to break the ice is to reach out and see if they will do something for you. Perhaps you can ask for a copy of their Annual Report or something else that would be appropriate. You may need to do some research but if you can ask them for an act of kindness, it can create a connection.

> *"The best rainmakers are just those that are most passionate about what they do. They believe more than everyone else that what they do matters, and they're good at it, and not shy about articulating that."*
>
> *– Mike Sheenan, CEO, Hill Holliday*

2.

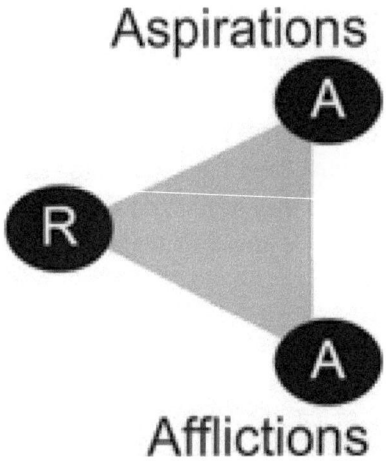

Aspirations

Afflictions

Once you've established rapport, you can then move on to figuring out what the prospect's current pain is and what they'd like to achieve in the future. Not only do you need to ask questions about their present circumstances but also about their future needs:

- "What keeps you up at night at the present time?
- "What are the key challenges facing your company?"
- "What aspects of your firm's current performance are you unhappy about"
- "Where do you hope to head as an organization in the future?"
- "What are the possibilities you can see?"

It's vital that you uncover both their current afflictions and what their aspirations are because this expands the value gap you're trying to quantify. Not only do you want to solve their problems but you also want to signal you can be an integral part of their bright future as well.

3.

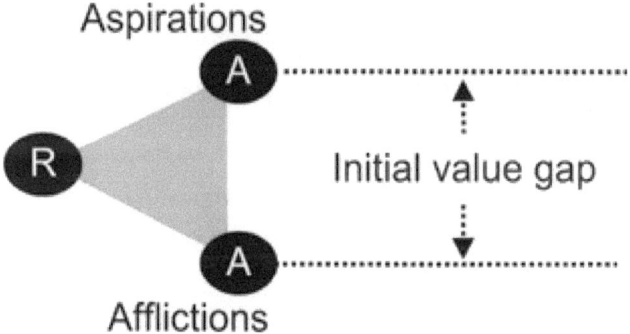

As a generalization, buyers usually start out in problem-solving mode. They will only go to the trouble of seeking out a solution when something bugs them enough to get them moving. They will usually have a clear view of the affliction and your challenge will be to not only solve that problem but also bring to the surface the other added value the solution will provide.

There are several things you can do to try and maximize that initial value gap.

- *Have a systematic approach to discovering needs* – sit

down and prepare a client needs analysis before you meet with them. Based on the industry they operate in, you can probably make an educated guess what kinds of needs they will have. You can adjust your analysis for special situations like acquisitions, the entry of new competitors into the market, next generation product launches and so forth. Think everything through in advance.

- *Ask probing questions* – which are concise and yet broad and open-ended. Watch as they answer for hints of a need or their lack of knowledge about what's required. Questions to try include:

  ° "How is your hiring process helping improve sales?"
  ° "How are you doing at retaining your best people?"
  ° "Is your sales manager doing a good job?"
  ° "Is your compensation structure working well?"

  Once you get an answer to these open-ended questions, you can then ask more detailed diagnostic questions and go from the general to the specific as you try to articulate what's happening.

- *Don't just probe, advocate* – bring research, examples of best practices, case studies and other expertise to the table as you speak with the prospect. Use this interaction time to help the prospect see there are new paths they could follow to reach their goals and that you will be a worthwhile resource moving forward.

- *If the discussion is stalling, try reversing direction* – if they suggest everything is rosy, you might say:

"Okay, well based on what I'm hearing, it sounds like things are working really well for you at the present time. If that's the case, I respect your time. If there's nothing for you to gain by discussing this further and everything is already where you want it to be, maybe we should stop now." Your abrupt change of direction will probably surprise them a little. It will force them to say "Well, there is one thing that maybe we should talk about a little more. We've noticed..." By indicating your awareness of the value of their time and offering to finish, you put them in the driver's seat. They will respect you more because of your up-front and direct approach as well. You rise above time-waster status.

4.

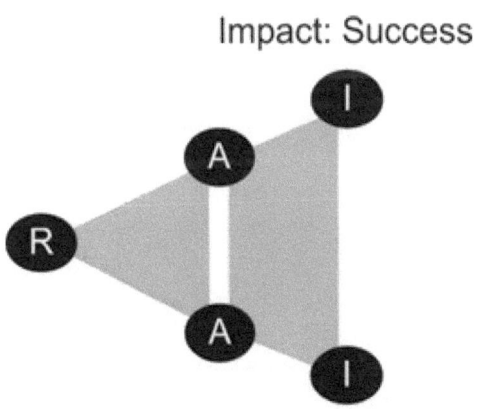

Impact: Success

Impact: Failure

Uncovering aspirations and afflictions is helpful and most salespeople leave it at that. Rainmakers move the conversation to the next level by figuring out the answer to the unstated question: "So what?" In other words, if the prospect's afflictions don't get resolved, what will happen then? If the prospect's aspirations don't become a reality, what future benefits will they miss out on?

"Answering 'So what?' will uncover the impact you can have on a customer's life and business. When you calculate the impact of helping prospects realize their aspirations and solve their afflictions, you establish a new baseline for where the prospects could be. When you understand the impact caused by prospects' afflictions, you establish the true business obstacles that they present. Take this all into account – the cost of failure and the benefits of success – and you have now established the true value gap."

– Mike Schultz and John Doerr

5.

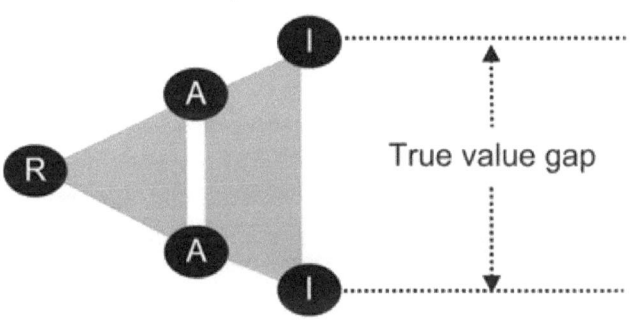

Impact: Success

True value gap

Impact: Failure

The impact of success and failure will come in two different flavors:

1. *Rational impact* – the type you can quantify in a business case. This is a matter of calculating the return-on-investment (ROI) of solving a problem or achieving as aspirational target in cash.
2. *Emotional impact* – where stress drops away or the excitement of being able to make a difference comes to the fore. What emotions will they feel if they pull off something spectacular?

If you can demonstrate the rational impact and make that tangible and within reach, you'll usually be able to take the prospect on an emotional journey which will build the emotional impact to desired levels. To make the true value gap as tangible and measurable as feasible, you should:

- *Calculate the rational impact in dollars* – develop an impact financial model which shows what the numbers will look like in that event. Put numbers to the financial benefits using reasonable assumptions.
- *Clarify the emotional impact* – things like increased prestige, reduced stress, more flexibility, etc.
- *Assess the impact of change versus maintaining the status quo* – clarify and put numbers to the opportunity cost of the status quo.
- *Build a sense of urgency for moving forward* – by making clear in the prospect's mind the amount of money which is being left on the table while a decision is not made. Get them to participate in a "What won't happen" analysis to make your case for moving forward immediately compelling.
- *Enhance your credibility* – by giving examples of other companies which have already realized these gains. The more well known that other entity is, the greater the credibility you'll build for yourself. Just the right case study here can have a powerful impact on their willingness to act now rather than waiting until next quarter, the next budget cycle or the next strategic review.

"The more you can make the impact tangible, the stronger the case for the impact will be. In essence, you need to paint a picture for them so they can see, as tangibly as you can depict it, what is going to change."

– Mike Schultz and John Doerr

6.

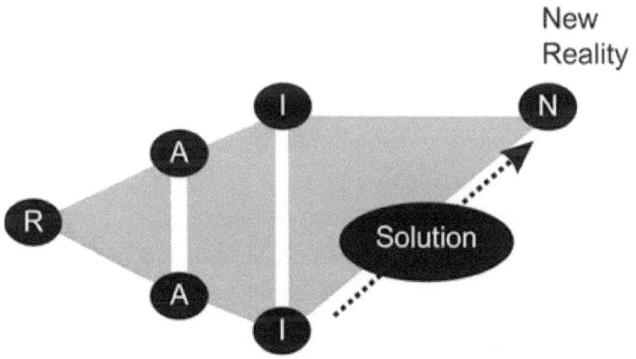

The last step in your RAIN sales conversation is to create in the mind of the prospect a new reality which is based on addressing their specific afflictions and realizing their preferred aspirations. You're trying to help them understand what they get when they buy and how their world will change – that is, the new reality you're hoping to create for them if they will just push the "Go" button.

This is really what you've been heading towards throughout the entire sales conversation. You use the information you've been gathering throughout to craft a solution which the prospect will immediately acknowledge would be a substantial gain. The art comes in translating that new reality into dollars and cents for the prospect, helping them see that solution is within reach and then committing them to get started on the journey immediately.

In practice, it's often feasible to communicate the new reality using a Before-and-After style chart. You specify:

- What life is like for the prospect at present.
- The new reality or future state they can get to if they implement your ideas.
- The phases or stages which will be required to make the transition. Here you can detail what you'll do, what the outcomes of each phase will be and how progress will be measured.
- The advantages of working with your firm versus your competitors or doing it themselves.
- The overall success metrics they agree should be used to measure success of the overall change initiative.
- The bottom line or core goal which is the top priority here so everyone is on the same page.

Based on what you know about the prospect, you can choose to emphasize some parts of the solution more strongly than others. Keep in mind buying is hard and sometimes it's difficult to visualize the impact and then choose between competing offers. By drawing a map in this way, you paint a picture for the buyer based on the RAIN approach. When the new reality is compelling and alluring, your prospect will want the solution, will know you're the best provider they can find and have confidence you can get the job done. It doesn't get any better than that for a salesperson.

Note rainmaking conversations require that you hit a good balance between advocacy and inquiry. In practice, this means if you talk too much, you'll make less sales than if you ask questions and listen. This can, however, be taken too far. If you ask question after question in the hopes that eventually some key demand will arise, your sales conversations will end up being long winded and aimless. The key is to be balancing advocacy (giving advice) and inquiry (finding out their true situation.)

Get into the habit of asking open-ended questions when you're with clients and listen to what they're saying judiciously. Tell them stories of other clients who were in similar situations to demonstrate your credibility without making a direct pitch. Develop active listening skills.

One other methodology which will help enhance your RAIN conversations is termed "The Five Whys." It's a simple yet powerful technique – when someone states a problem, ask them "why" that came about. Keep doing that five times for all the points they bring out and you'll get to the root cause of what's going on. The Five Whys ensure you're focusing on fixing the underlying cause rather than just a symptom. To illustrate:

Problem: The production line has stopped again!

#1: Why did the production line stop?
Answer: A piece of equipment blew a fuse.
#2: Why did that equipment blow a fuse?
Answer: Because the bearings were overheating.
#3: Why did the bearings overheat?
Answer: Because they had insufficient lubrication.
#4: Why were the bearings not lubricated?
Answer: Nobody remembered to oil them.
#5: Why did nobody oil them?
Answer: We don't have a maintenance schedule.
#6: Why isn't there a maintenance schedule?
Answer: Silence
To make RAIN conversations work, you've got to drill down by asking why questions at least five times to get to the root causes.

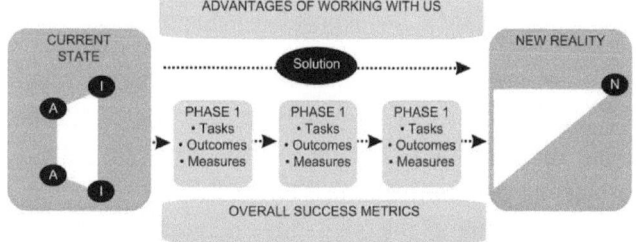

BOTTOM LINE – Our Core Goal _____
_____

3. FOUR KEYS TO SUCCESS FOR RAIN SELLING

Companies and individuals which achieve higher results than others with RAIN conversations do so because they focus on RASP:

R *Role readiness* – be prepared to succeed

A *Action* – execute on activities which lead to sales

S *Skills & knowledge* – know how and what you sell

P *Processes* – have a framework for results

R: *ROLE READINESS* – BE PREPARED TO SUCCEED

When you're role ready, you have the skills and knowledge you need to succeed. You understand the drivers of sales success and minimize anything which would detract from your influence.

For RAIN selling, you'll be role ready when you have this mindset:

- I will get the prospect's attention by being memorable, by highlighting my firm's differentiation and by employing useful attention-grabbing marketing activities.

- I will pique the prospect's attention by helping them visualize what they're missing. I will help them see the value gap and offer a solution which closes it.
- I will stoke the prospect's desire to change his or her reality by uncovering needs, sharing examples of success stories to follow and by helping them see the benefits of that new reality.
- I understand envy is desire with a turbo boost. I will therefore draw word pictures of what achieving that new reality will mean so the prospect feels compelled to take action immediately.
- I realize prospects need to go on an emotional journey throughout the sales process. Therefore, I tell stories which will help prospects form positive mental images, feel connected to powerful emotions and elicit strong responses.
- I understand the importance of providing proof (product demonstrations) to prospects of the benefits of what I have to offer. By increasing belief, I reduce risks and inspire action.
- I realize people buy with their hearts and then justify with their heads. To help prospects buy, I provide them with information they can use to explain their return-on-investment (ROI) to others.
- I make it easy for people to trust me. I do this by always playing for a win-win, by refusing to compromise my integrity, by being transparent and by always doing

what I say I'm going to do.

- I provide a series of stepping stones for people to get used to dealing with me. Buying is a leap of faith and to shorten that leap, I use either a domino strategy (easy first step) or a layering strategy (up-sell).
- I will help the prospect feel responsible for their own decision. To get the prospect to take ownership, I will uncover their afflictions, aspirations and impact.
- I will actively involve prospects in helping develop solutions to their problems. If I enlist the prospect in helping craft a solution, they will be more inclined to move forward in the purchasing process.
- I understand people feel the need to be included in what others are doing. Testimonials provide validation and confirmation which is helpful. I will use social proof in all its forms to stoke their desire.
- I realize people are attracted to rarity. They don't want to miss opportunities. Thus, I will highlight loss of opportunity which may arise if they don't act now.
- I know people pay attention to and ultimately buy from someone they like. I will try and be likeable.
- While I'm passionate about what I offer, I'm not needy. If the sale does not add value for the prospect, I'm ready and willing to walk away. I focus on value to the buyer.
- I'm not afraid to ask for a commitment to move forward in writing and in a public setting. I understand when people have committed publicly, there's more pressure for them to follow through and do what they said. I ask

for commitments at the right time.

To make sales, you've got to get your attitude right first and then everything else will follow.

A: *ACTION* – EXECUTE ON ACTIVITIES WHICH LEAD TO SALES

> *"We've seen more people intend to become top performers in sales than those who actually do it."*
>
> — *Mike Schultz and John Doerr*

When it comes to making sales, action is a very simple concept. Success is a matter of doing the right amount of the right things effectively:

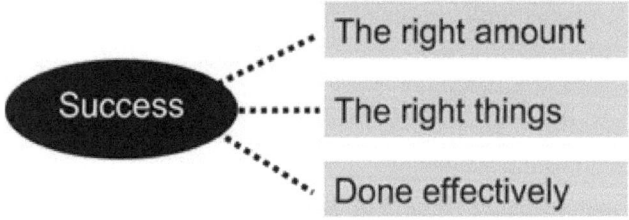

- *The right amount* – Most salespeople can get more done each day if they engage in regular planning. This is a matter of setting activity targets, large picture goals and then disciplining yourself to fill each day with productive activity. Spending 5 percent of your time on planning can make the other 95 percent much more productive.

- *The right things* – Keep asking: "Am I doing the things right now which will help me achieve my goals faster?" For most salespeople, filling the front-end of their pipeline is their most important action but it's common for this to be given a low priority. Don't let this get relegated to the last thing you want to do each day. Discipline yourself to do the right things. Set goals (big picture, three- to five-year, next 12 months) and then break them down into what needs to get done today.

- *Done effectively* – If you're making the right amount of calls and speaking to the right people but nothing is happening, that's an indicator you need to learn more so you can become more effective.

> *"The road to success is always under repair. Live by goals and you won't get lost on the side streets, wondering to yourself why you're not there yet. Creating a rainmaking conversation takes action. Leading a rainmaking conversation takes action. Converting a conversation into a sale ... You get the idea."*
>
> *– Mike Schultz and John Doerr*

S: *SKILLS & KNOWLEDGE* – KNOW HOW AND WHAT YOU SELL

You can't take action and sell more if you don't have the requisite skills and knowledge base. Learn how to:

- *Create rainmaking conversations over the phone* – which always comes down to articulating what's-in-it-for-me to the customer. The six basic approaches which work for telephone calls, e-mails and sales letters are where you offer them a chance to learn more are:

  - ° How others have solved a problem in the past.
  - ° How you achieved something noteworthy.
  - ° A new idea which have just become available.
  - ° An innovative approach for solving a problem.
  - ° A nonthreatening first step they can take.
  - ° You communicate how you add value.

  Learn how to use and how to benefit from each of these approaches and then get calling prospects and using them. The best way to learn how to do this better is to take the plunge and start calling.
- *Handle objections constructively* – which usually arise when there is no trust, no need, no urgency or no money on the part of the prospect. To handle an objection constructively, use the tried and true five-step formula:

  - ° Listen carefully to the objection and fight the urge to respond immediately

- ° Ask them a few questions to make sure you understand the real issue
- ° Respond succinctly and directly to the underlying issues and concerns
- ° Confirm with them whether your answer takes care of that issue
- ° Continue forward with your RAIN conversation and get back to selling

> *"Objections are barriers, but they are also buying signals. Objections are clear signals that you have more work to do in the selling process."*
>
> *– Mike Schultz and John Doerr*

- *Close sales* – which is the only way a deal will move forward and get actioned. Closing is always a risky process and your job is to help the buyer work through everything that's involved. As long as you're acting ethically in their best interests, closing is like a checklist you work through one issue at a time:

  - ° Have I addressed all the RAIN elements by building rapport, understanding their aspirations and afflictions, clarifying the impact of success and coming up with a viable solution?
  - ° Is the buyer FAINT qualified – do they have the financial capacity and authority to make a decision, are they interested, do they understand the need for your solution and is the timing right for a sale?

- ° Do I understand the decision-making process as it exists in this organization?
- ° Has the buyer indicated a preference for my solution and that he/she will make a decision relatively promptly?
- ° Is the buyer aware of the likely price range and delivery time-frame?
- ° Have I succeeded in differentiating my solution from those offered by competitors?
- ° Can I have the chance to present my solution in person so I can build the relationship and be part of the decision making process?
- ° Do I have complete confidence my solution is the best way forward and the best solution if the buyer and I were to reverse roles?
- ° Have I clearly communicated the next step forward for the prospect?
- ° Am I genuinely willing to walk away if we cannot reach agreement on price?
- ° Are we really talking about a clear-cut win-win outcome here?

If you take the time and effort to make certain your deal is close ready before you start closing, then you increase and enhance your chances of success. Work your way steadily through the checklist.

P: *PROCESSES* – HAVE A FRAMEWORK FOR RESULTS

Rainmakers always have a system or framework which helps them take those actions which will achieve the best possible sales results. In other words, they have processes which are systematic approaches to follow.

Rainmaking conversations generally follow eight stages where you need to be aware of what a prospect is thinking in each. The stages are:

Rapport	Do I like this person?
Conversation	Is he/she organized & competent?
Interest	Does he/she understand my needs?
Impact	What is the ROI?
New reality	Is the approach credible?
Buy process	Should I get others involved?
Next steps	Are there reasons to continue?
Followup	Will I commit to move forward?

Be fully aware of the conversation stage which is taking place inside your prospect's head at the moment and follow the RAIN roadmap. Make sure you're taking a systematic approach to sales rather than leaving it to hit-and-miss techniques.

4. THE 10 RAINMAKER PRINCIPLES

Following the RAIN road map will help you sell effectively but if you really want to achieve and join the ranks of the elite, there are 10 Rainmaker Principles you need to take to heart and then apply:

1. ALWAYS PLAY TO WIN-WIN

Rainmakers always respect and try to satisfy the best interests of their clients as well as their own. You have to exhibit the hustle, passion and intensity of an elite performer but never lose sight of serving your prospect's best interests to be a rainmaker.

2. LIVE BY GOALS

Rainmakers are fanatical about setting goals and achieving them. To excel as a rainmaker, make setting goals and then evaluating your performance a part of your daily rituals. Live and breathe your goals.

3. TAKE ACTION

All rainmakers are proactive. They don't sit back and wait for people to come to them. Remind yourself frequently goals without actions won't get you far at all. Get into the habit of being in action. Let other people stop at merely having good intentions.

4. THINK ABOUT BUYING FIRST, SELLING SECOND

Rainmakers habitually look at the buying process through their customer's eyes. They map their selling processes to the processes and psychology of buying. They understand what's going on in their prospect's minds and adjust accordingly. To become a rainmaker, look at things from the buyer's perspective.

5. KNOW WHAT YOU NEED TO KNOW TO SELL

Rainmakers are experts. They have deep market knowledge, know their customer's needs in detail, understand their own products and services, and have an accurate sense of their value. You don't have to be a technical expert in every field to be a rainmaker but you do need to know what you must know to sell.

6. CREATE NEW CONVERSATIONS EVERY DAY

Rainmakers are constantly feeding the front of their sales pipeline. They also work to improve the quality of their new prospects all the time. Make it your goal to never let a day pass without speaking to your referral sources with the intent of sourcing new business.

7. LEAD PRODUCTIVE CONVERSATIONS

Rainmakers know how to conduct conversations which range from prospecting to needs discovery to closing to support and account management. Learn how to conduct masterful conversations in each of these areas. You won't be a rainmaker until you do.

8. SET THE AGENDA AND BE A CHANGE AGENT

Rainmakers make recommendations, provide prospects with sound advice and assist. Another way of saying this is rainmakers are change agents. They're not afraid to push when it's in their client's best interests for them to do so. Be prepared and be ready so you can make the right things happen.

9. EXHIBIT COURAGE

Rainmakers have courage. They rise to the occasion. To do the same, conquer your fears and work towards winning the most productive sales opportunities whenever and wherever they arise. And don't forget to be prepared to ride out the challenges which will come along.

10. ASSESS, GET FEEDBACK AND IMPROVE

Rainmakers are anxious to learn the cold, hard truth about how they're performing. Welcome and seek feedback from everyone you interact with. Then get to work building on what's good and changing what's bad. This development cycle never ends so make it work in your favor and not against you.

> *"You are the only person who can determine your success. Just as you need buyers to take ownership of their decisions and their agendas, it is up to you to take ownership of your actions and do all you can to make your sales conversations bear fruit. No excuses."*
>
> *– Mike Schultz and John Doerr*

> *"Knowledge is the food of the soul."*
>
> *– Plato*

> *"I've always found the harder I worked, the better my luck was."*
>
> *– Ed Bradley*

> *"We suggest that you take the 10 Rainmaker Principles and post them on the wall in your workspace in an area where you can see them and read them once each day. Read them every day and they'll affect how you think. How you think will affect how you act. And how you act... well, that's the key to reaching your rainmaking destiny."*
>
> *– Mike Schultz and John Doerr*

"We wrote Rainmaking Conversations for salespeople, business leaders, professionals, and anyone who wants to create and lead masterful sales conversations – conversations that fill the pipeline, win new deals, and create the greatest opportunities for the largest, most secure, and most profitable accounts. RAIN, RASP, and the 10 Rainmaker Principles form the core of the RAIN Selling method – the training and development program we at RAIN Group employ to help companies create dramatic improvements in sales performance and to help individuals become top-performing rainmakers.

– Mike Schultz and John Doerr